A Hatfield Mass

A HATFIELD MASS

voice and shape in an English landscape

Martyn Crucefix

First published in 2014 by
Worple Press
Achill Sound, 2b Dry Hill Road
Tonbridge
Kent TN9 1LX.
www.worplepress.co.uk

© Copyright Martyn Crucefix

The moral right of the author has been asserted in accordance with the Copyrights, Designs and Patents Act of 1988. All rights reserved.

Cover image, Draped Reclining Figure (LH 336), by Henry Moore

No part of this work covered by the copyright thereon may be reproduced or used in any means – graphic, electronic, or mechanical, including copying, recording, taping, or information storage or retrieval systems – without written permission of the publisher.

Printed by imprintdigital
Upton Pyne, Exeter
www.imprintdigital.net

Typeset by narrator
www.narrator.me.uk
info@narrator.me.uk
033 022 300 39

ISBN: 978-1-905208-25-8

Acknowledgements

The exhibition of Henry Moore sculptures which initiated this sequence of poems took place in the grounds of Hatfield House, Hertfordshire, from April to September, 2011. The pieces named are a small selection of what was on show in the gardens and woodlands surrounding the house.

The pieces referred to in the text are: Large Totem Head (LH 577); Three Piece Reclining Figure Draped (LH 655); Reclining Figure, Angles (LH 675); Draped Reclining Figure (LH 336); Mother and Child (LH 269b); Reclining Connected Forms (LH 612) with other images relating to Reclining Mother and Child (LH 649).

The coda section of the sequence is a loose version of the anonymous German libretto of Bach's cantata 'Ich habe genug…' (BWV 82).

'*La beauté un regret, l'oeuvre ne prendre*
À pleines mains qu'une eau qui se refuse'
Yves Bonnefoy, 'De Vent et de Fumée', *La Vie errante* (1993)

'. . . *repeated in a finer tone and so repeated*'
John Keats, *To Benjamin Bailey*, 22nd November, 1817

Contents

1. Large Totem Head 1
2. Three Piece Reclining Figure, Draped 6
3. Reclining Figure, Angles 10
4. Draped Reclining Figure 12
5. Mother and Child 16
6. Reclining Connected Forms 18
6. A voice singing 23

1. Large Totem Head
kyrie

This the head I had at twenty
though I'd be as much a fool to credit it now

not try to translate so quickly—
instead reach behind to where in life
the finest hairs curled
to run my fingers down the brazen neck

to begin again
to begin again

to contemplate the 'cyclops' the 'helmet head'
the sensation of my hand
where it strokes
my own not any other's neck

till the bolt disappearing down my spine—
it is only myself I am consoling

save me
save me

Then think myself more capable now
when there may be minutes on end

when all's elastic
and flex and accommodation

more capable of strolling this clipped avenue
under the gaze of this tilted head

in what looks like anticipation—
of taking note of the wren's tick-ticking

the wren's snicker animating the hedge
the chink of a blackbird in the holly tree

as a trickle of dry gravel shifts beneath
the walking-pace of passing tyres

a crackling beneath each suspended weight—
these are visitors whose brief passing

is marked by little lateral explosions
engines growling beyond the thickness

beyond the day-long darkness of yew hedge

Yet pale dust kicked up only yesterday
only yesterday while I walked

save me
save me

This morning greying dampness instead
differently to conjure a different air

till this is perhaps hardly a head at all
rather something hollowed like a shell

a pod lobed and upright—a closer match
to this morning's tentative breeze

to the perfume from blooming rose-beds
where they are being dug in accordance

with the season's shift of temperatures
where sunlight exchanges its tans for gold

I try inexorably I try too hard
till the lobes of lucid presence fall away
to a niche to some recess of myself

in fragments it swills and fills it empties
its brief shavings smoothly
into the shell of my head—it is a deluge
where they circulate to and fro

be still
be still

O let this passing be

let go unencumbered down the long avenue
moving to wordlessness without end—

let this be translated here to something
years later I must have stumbled upon

2. Three Piece Reclining Figure, Draped
gloria

for Louise

Nothing whatsoever to do with dissolution
nor decay this falling to pieces

familiar from my walking out in pieces
as I do in the course of most of my days

Though she is half-covered she seems one
with these stumps and blocks of legs

draped with nothing more round her thick thighs
like the trunks of golden-barked trees

where the knee's articulation is the object
I gaze at I want to lick so much

where slicing through the body my hands go
burrow and under and between the air

O she has the long broad back I reach for
by night your shallow-ribbed back

these holes suggestive of hands-on-hip
as if she's propped herself in our morning bed

and this other is the hole of the heart
defined by curves replete with daylight

with gardens and lawns haunted by flesh
real and weighty and rounded and plinthed

and yours by sunrise after the night before
the angle of my crooked arm frames your breast

under the high-held leaves of oak and ash

In that moment we've such bodies as have
slipped their limits to stretch and curve

to define the air by losing self-definition
where crows and jays flap their untidy rags

no longer mocking the pared-back stump
of the head—now set to praise the sun

with these minuscule pocks and scratches
these distinguishing marks from top to toe

and her broad back flat-ribbed and stroked
is yours as over one shoulder I look for day

to rise over the other where I lay my head

3. Reclining Figure, Angles
credo

If there must be a word
and believe me there must
then it is the word alert

and drawn to what moves
beyond her—where she lies
draped about the knees

with fabric pulled taut again
a way of explaining time
to the eternal moment

as her left leg declines
though no longer passive—
the turn of her left shoulder

towards a strong focal point
leaves the body twisted
on the thrust of her flat-

planted right foot—image
of awareness repeatedly
alertness of an interest in

though there's nothing
here of the egotistical—
in these graceful airs

in what passes through
as it has through these others
the flex and curve

of self-confident pride
yet hollowed and smoothed
and though the head

is shaped to a feature
still the magisterial gaze
is blankly all-seeing

staring beyond shock
or surprise or pleasure
or anger or envy forever

beyond grief—this curious
taking notice and if it ever
comes to be diminished

I mean the head on its stump
it's the body that senses
and nothing's let slip

4. Draped Reclining Figure
sanctus

Covered in such a delicate material
her spreading knees bring tension to the pose
and set me thinking of cheese-cloth skirts

have me reviving forty years ago
all wrapped round widely-scissored knees
in something of the pose of parturition

Or better still nine months before
as she readies again to pull up her hem
to receive a man—it's as if here

where the drying beech-mast moves today
rolling under my slow-moving feet
in the beech tree that rises beside her

luminous and wide stands the universe
where choices made cannot be re-made

It's this criss-cross of already-laden years
that compels these images to rise—
here the sofa always to her right-hand side

beneath her elbows and her lovely arse
the carpet that soon must have burned
those little blushes across our skin

until her left hand begins to worry it—
this the opening of the long afterwards
where the carpet unrolls beneath me too

where I'm slumped prone and panting

Begin this unpicking loops of red and green
almost the green of these grass blades
while to her left stands the coffee table

we'd shoved to one side in need of space
and beyond her stiffly inclining head
the Dansette is purring still

with its lid up its turntable running
where the needle tut-tuts at having done
with 'Song of the Wind' its passionate whispering

and see my gaze declining my laden head
before the onslaught in her limbs
as she invites—though forty years have gone—

she reaches down to lift her hem once more
as if she wants me more like a proper man

5. Mother and Child
bendictus

for Antonia and Anne

Then sing this blessing
sing this heft of flesh
to the air where surgically
sun cuts the canopy
of an old English wood

where the ways are scrapings
through untidy litter
of leaves and plantings
last year's re-establishing
its roots and this yields

parables of absent fathers
whose weakened faith
lies in one strong arm
as if that were enough
to be rid of all doubt—

yet see what remains
the tiny gleam of black ant
traversing the plinth
beneath the mother's gaze
hair bound on her head

and this encircling arc
of her cradle-arms
is more speech than fear
and her lunging forward
is to laugh as she has

scooped up her boy-child
from his perilous flight
with two powerful hands
with two powerful hands
singing praise giving thanks

his bold outward glance
as a russet-brown blackbird
swoops before them—
O fathers you must better
this one armed embrace

6. Reclining Connected Forms
agnus dei

Love—your broad flat-ribbed length of back
makes angles to the rhododendron bloom
to the red framing that for a matter of days
is gorged and sun-shot

and within a week the stringy stamens
are browned the remains of petals shrivelling
like burnt crusts to burnt umber—

still the Lyme-shaped harbour of your shadow
has the shell-like chess-piece of the child
transfixed by the bolt of a mother's arm

She is all pointed breasts all musculature
and trunk-thick thighs yet unaware
of her feet because she does not intend
for now to travel any further—and this

despite these visitors in passing groups
who stroll and drift to a halt
murmuring *ugly child what an ugly child*—

but the child is ugly
because it has a long way to go
and if not more beautiful we grow more rich

And this is something I have sometimes known
coming across the meadows they have let go
to become shaggy and bright
coming through flowering grasses

through purple vetch and yellow vetch erect
over last year's browned remains
of oak leaf and beech-mast and beech leaf

strolling with my head sluiced and hollowed
cleared for rain as much as sun
for fleet days in pursuit of these fading nights

In the strictest of series—yet always becoming
the present becoming the past
to the vanishing point of her smile
the squeal of laughter at what has gone

yet never completely gone—
what has shape and expires to shapelessness
to which we give words against all wordlessness

what seems womb as much as coffin
and inside lying the shape of child to come
the growing child become sullen teenager

Become this twenty-year-old and perhaps
sometime father determined to consider
the head and bone and something of wings—
O pelvic bone

where my fingers come to rest
at this shelter this entrance this remarkable exit
shape of coffin as much as womb

since what one night utterly destroys us
sets out light-footed to put a girdle round the world
returning only to re-make us at dawn

6. A voice singing
coda

Now I have enough—
what thrives on hope and faith
cradled in my embrace
now I have enough

of vivid present lucid sight
pressed upon my heart
each instant in delight
come—the moment to depart

Now I have enough—
assurance gleaned from this alone
that I am yours and you my own

embracing you for truth
with Simeon I gaze I murmur
of joys to come—

then set me with him in pursuit
O would you loose me let me further
overcoming outworn limit

readied for my departure—
in rapture sing to you to earth
now I have enough

Tumble eyelids on weary eyes
one soft descent one moment's repose

O world—I can wait no longer
in this place where nothing further

will exercise my soul—
to linger here is to petrify

there—more and more to uncover—
sweetness richer to fulfill

O love—to hear that looked for Now!
that instant motion spurred at once

this running into the world's finer sand
this vanishing in your embrace—

here—here my leaving close at hand
then greet the world goodnight and now

There is such joy in each little death
I'm ready—then approach the moment—

this loosening—of each gathered limit
for fear it—confines me from the earth

Note

Rimbaud suggests our openness to life, the unearned pleasures of the child, begin to close off around the age of seven. The rigidity of the maturing self, the closing in of solipsism is something from which these poems look to be rescued or relieved. Salvation lies in the movement towards flexure with or accommodation of the world about us, the subjective becoming interconnected, melded with the objective world.

One of the occasions in which this is experienced is physical love, the engaging with and knowing of another's body, in which we emerge from the limits of self into the solids and spaces of another, the loss of self re-defining the other. This only takes place during time (the cessation of duration becomes a form of pornographic experience – a false idealising of something that must remain transient).

The fuel of such re-organisation of perception is attentivenesss which the poems think of as desire and is held in tension with the temptations and indeed necessities of conceptual thought which work to stop the passage of time and affirm a dream which the body can never really know.

To achieve something, for some while, of openness to the plenitude of full presence is felt as blessing and this is imaged as maternal and perhaps really is more maternal than paternal. The outcome of experiences of this kind is an out-wardness of the developing individual as opposed to the solipsistic confinements – the cyclops and helmet heads – of earlier poems.

The development of the child into adulthood is a process through duration of increasing richness of experience in which the criterion of openness is most important. Such a process of becoming demands we accommodate always our own 'demise' as we move from one state to another.

The original of the coda of songs refers to the Biblical figure Simeon, told by the Holy Spirit that he would not die before he had seen the new born Jesus. His prayer on seeing Christ was

"Lord, now you let your servant depart in peace, according to your word; for my eyes have seen your salvation". The poems intend to secularise this to a celebration of the passing of one form of self into the next since to linger here is to petrify and risk a return to the prison-like state of solipsism.